2491

2/86

JUN 10 '06

SEP 08

2491

GRASSLANDS

Troll Associates

GRASSLANDS

by Louis Sabin

Illustrated by James Watling

Troll Associates

Library of Congress Cataloging in Publication Data

Sabin, Louis.
  Grasslands.

  Summary: Discusses the types of grasslands, their
uses, and their fauna.
    1. Grassland ecology—Juvenile literature.   [1. Grass-
lands.   2. Grassland animals]   I. Watling, James, ill.
II. Title.
QH541.5.P7S3   1984   574.5′2643   84-2661
ISBN 0-8167-0214-4 (lib. bdg.)
ISBN 0-8167-0215-2 (pbk.)

The grasslands stretch as far as the eye can see. Like a calm dry ocean, they are nearly flat, with only a few gentle rises here and there. There are no jagged outcroppings of rock, no tall trees, no deep canyons or valleys. For as far as you can see in all directions, the view is clear. There is nothing but a vast, endless sea of grass.

There are three types of grasslands—the steppes, the prairies, and the savannas.

Steppes have short grasses, because they are found in a semi-arid climate with hot summers and cold winters. Most of the American Great Plains is this kind of grassland.

Prairies have tall grasses, and more humid climates than steppes. Much of the American midwest was once this kind of grassland. But today, much of the tall grass has been plowed under and replaced with cereal crops, such as wheat.

Savannas are tropical grasslands with dry winters and wet summers. Coarse grasses grow on the savannas. The Sudan in Africa is an example of a tropical savanna.

At one time, many millions of years ago, there were no grasslands on our planet. Where the grasslands are today, there were once lowlands filled with water.

Then came a series of ice ages—long periods of time when the temperature all over the world was very low. Huge seas of ice, called glaciers, covered much of the Earth's surface. Then the temperature rose again, melting the glaciers.

As the glaciers melted, water ran down

the great mountain ranges. It carried sediment, or bits of rocks and minerals, as it flowed into the lowlands. The sediment built up in these lowland basins, and in time, became rich soil. Seeds took root in the soil; and before long, the land was rich with grass.

The climate of the grasslands can vary greatly from season to season. Winters may be very cold, with large amounts of snowfall and strong, freezing winds. Summers may be unbearably hot. In the Great Plains of North America, summer often brings driving, twisting winds called tornados and hailstorms that pelt the land with balls of ice as large as your fist.

The weather can also vary greatly from year to year. There may be a number of years with a moderate amount of rainfall and a moderate amount of sunshine. In these years, the tall grasses grow rich and thick.

But then there may be several years of drought, when almost no rain falls. Now the tall grasses cannot thrive. Only the short grasses have enough moisture to grow. And if the drought lasts long enough, only scattered clumps of hardy short grasses may survive.

A long drought in the grasslands turns the top layer of soil to dust. The winds that sweep across the grasslands whip the dust into the air. This kind of drought ravaged the Great Plains of North America in the early part of the twentieth century. It turned the fertile grasslands into an immense, barren "dust bowl." The land seemed to be covered by a powdery gray blanket, and even the air was so heavy with dust that the sunshine was blotted out.

When drought conditions, like those that caused the dust bowl, continue for many years, grasslands can turn into deserts. Fortunately, however, droughts do not usually last more than a few years. In time, the rains return, and the seeds that have been lying in the ground take root. Soon the grasslands are lush and healthy again.

Grasslands are covered with many different kinds of grasses. Some—the short grasses such as buffalo grass and blue grama—grow in the driest regions of the grasslands.

Where there is more rainfall, the middle-sized grasses take over. These include the split-beard blue stem, needle grass, and June grass.

And on grasslands where the most rain falls, the towering tall grasses grow. These include Indian grass, switch grass, and tall blue stem, which grows taller than the tallest human beings.

All of the different kinds of grasses have complicated root systems that are very important to the life of the grasslands. The roots of the tall blue stem, for example, reach down about six feet, or two meters, into the ground. And there are grasses that have roots that go down twice as far!

June grass

Indian grass

Big blue stem

Needle grass

Little blue grass

21

The thick, deep tangle of grass roots carries water and minerals up to the growing plants. The roots also hold the soil in place. And every year, when winter kills the grass, this also helps the grasslands. The dead matter decays and adds nutrients to the soil. This rich soil feeds new plants.

Grasslands are more than just the home of growing plants. They are also rich in animal life of all kinds. In the summer, the grasslands teem with butterflies and moths, bees, wasps, flies, aphids, beetles, and many other insects. They live off the grasses, and they serve as food for other insects, birds, and animals.

23

Many of the insects also perform an important job for the grasslands. As they move from one plant to another, they carry pollen. This pollen fertilizes the plants so that new crops of grass will grow.

No grassland insect is more important or more numerous than the grasshopper. Birds and animals of the grasslands eat grasshoppers, which feed on plant life. These insects spend almost all their lives eating plants.

In years when there is a lot of rain, the grasshopper population is small, and they are no problem for the grasslands. But when there is a long dry spell, the grasshopper population increases, and does great damage to the plant life.

One kind of short-horned grasshopper, called the locust, has been feared throughout history because of the way it destroys all the vegetation in an area. These locusts fly great distances in huge swarms, come down, consume an entire field, and fly on. The plague of locusts described in the Bible is about a species of short-horned grass-hoppers.

The grasslands are also home for many small seed-eating and insect-eating birds, as well as the larger, predatory birds. Among the winged predators, or hunters, are eagles, hawks, and falcons. They feed on squirrels, jack rabbits, mice, voles, and other small animals.

Burrowing animals are especially plentiful in the grasslands. These include moles, pocket gophers, thirteen-lined ground squirrels, badgers, and prairie deer mice.

There is even a bird that lives under the ground. It is called the burrowing owl, but it doesn't dig its own burrow. Instead, it lives in the burrow that was once the home of a prairie dog.

The prairie dog is not a dog at all, but a small rodent with brown or yellow-gray fur. It gets its name from the short "yip" it makes, which sounds something like a dog's bark. Prairie dogs eat grassland vegetation and live in underground communities that are like small towns.

Prairie dogs are among the most social of all animals. They are also helpful to the grasslands. Their tunnels help oxygen and water to circulate throughout the soil.

The larger animals living in the grasslands include deer and elk, wolves and coyotes. Huge herds of bison, or American buffalo, once grazed the American grasslands. Before their numbers were drastically reduced by hunters, they provided food and clothing for the Plains Indians and the early settlers.

Today, grasslands the world over are used to produce food for people. Some are grazing lands for cattle, sheep, and goats, which provide us with meat and dairy products. And some are covered with grain —endless fields of wheat, rye, barley, and corn. These crops are used to feed livestock, to make cereals, and to make flour for baked goods of all kinds.

Still other grasslands remain as they have
for centuries—stretching endlessly, as far as
the eye can see. They are like vast open
seas...but they are seas of grass.